My Two Homes

Julie Murray

Abdo Kids Junior
is an Imprint of Abdo Kids
abdobooks.com

THIS IS MY FAMILY

abdobooks.com

Published by Abdo Kids, a division of ABDO, P.O. Box 398166, Minneapolis, Minnesota 55439.
Copyright © 2021 by Abdo Consulting Group, Inc. International copyrights reserved in all countries.
No part of this book may be reproduced in any form without written permission from the publisher.
Abdo Kids Junior™ is a trademark and logo of Abdo Kids.

Printed in the United States of America, North Mankato, Minnesota.

052020

092020

THIS BOOK CONTAINS
RECYCLED MATERIALS

Photo Credits: iStock, Shutterstock

Production Contributors: Teddy Borth, Jennie Forsberg, Grace Hansen

Design Contributors: Candice Keimig, Pakou Moua, Dorothy Toth

Library of Congress Control Number: 2019955562

Publisher's Cataloging-in-Publication Data

Names: Murray, Julie, author.

Title: My two homes / by Julie Murray

Description: Minneapolis, Minnesota : Abdo Kids, 2021 | Series: This is my family | Includes online
    resources and index.

Identifiers: ISBN 9781098202255 (lib. bdg.) | ISBN 9781644943939 (pbk.) | ISBN 9781098203238 (ebook)
    | ISBN 9781098203726 (Read-to-Me ebook)

Subjects: LCSH: Families--Juvenile literature. | Home--Juvenile literature. | Children of separated parents—
    Juvenile literature. | Children of divorced parents--Juvenile literature. | Families--Social aspects—
    Juvenile literature.

Classification: DDC 306.85--dc23

Table of Contents

My Two Homes

Some kids have two homes.
They split their time
between them.

Lou eats at his mom's house.

They make soup.

Jane sleeps at her dad's condo. She shares a room with her sister.

Nathan is at his mom's apartment. He helps her paint.

Abby rides the bus. She gets picked up at her dad's house.

13

Cara is swimming with her sister. They are at their mom's house.

Eva has a dog. Buster stays at her dad's townhome.

Seth **studies** at his mom's house.

She helps him with his math.

Ken plants flowers. It makes his dad's house look nice.

Some Different Kinds of Homes

apartment

condo

house

townhome

Glossary

study
to try to learn.

townhome
a home that is part of a row of similar homes. It is connected to other homes by shared walls.

Index

Abdo Kids
ONLINE
FREE! ONLINE MULTIMEDIA RESOURCES

Visit **abdokids.com** to access crafts, games, videos, and more!

Use Abdo Kids code
TMK2255
or scan this QR code!